PROMOTING MENTAL MATHEMATICS

The need to promote mental mathematics has received a lot of curriculum attention in recent years, particularly in terms of providing children with opportunities to discuss the methods that they use. Research* shows that allowing children to explain their mental processes verbally can have a positive effect on their achievements: factual and conceptual knowledge is increased and there is often a marked improvement in pupil confidence. Many teachers now build in time for class or group discussion of mental strategies.

There remains a need, however, for individual consolidation of these strategies. With a whole class to manage, it can be difficult to ensure that each child has an opportunity to explain his or her ideas. Traditionally, many commercial maths schemes present number activities in such a way that the practice of a taught written algorithm is implicit; they do not build on the *mental strategies* that the teacher has been promoting.

CHILDREN TALKING AND WRITING ABOUT THEIR MATHS

Children need to acquire a mathematical vocabulary if they are to become effective mathematicians and have access to the maths problems they encounter in school and outside. This language must be developed systematically. A photocopiable list of some of the mathematical vocabulary that this age group should be using when reflecting on the activities in this book is given on page 6. This list may be particularly valuable for children whose first language is not English. You may also like to refer to the National Numeracy Project booklet *Mathematical Vocabulary* (BEAM).

While children need written maths practice, they also need opportunities to rehearse their developing mental strategies individually. Hence you will find a strong emphasis in these activity sheets on children writing, or talking to each other, about *how* they have done particular calculations or *why* they have reached certain conclusions. This reflection will consolidate the learning, so it is important to value these sections of the sheets. The children's own shorthand terms and phrases are acceptable in this context.

Various classroom strategies could be used to encourage the children to reflect on their maths. These might include: maths-talk partners – with whom to share ideas and answers; adult support – using classroom assistants, or encouraging parents, to talk to the children about their maths work;

maths diaries – for the ch... classroom mathematical ... to reflect on their own wo... sessions – either in groups, ... carpet time, where childre... ...their notes and discuss their mental maths strategies.

KNOWING KEY FACTS

Nothing slows down children's development in mental strategies as severely as not having adequate quick recall of the necessary number facts. The activities in this book encourage children to use and apply the facts they already know and to build upon them. For example, a Year 3/Primary 4 child might work out that since 48 + 10 is 58, 48 + 9 is 57 (see page 16).

It is essential to check first that children undertaking these activities have a secure store of relevant facts or quick ways of figuring them out; an appropriate test is given on photocopiable page 7 (answers on page 2). A child who completes this test confidently should be ready to tackle the activities in this book.

HOW TO USE THE ACTIVITY SHEETS

These activities reflect recent research* into commonly used mental strategies, and have been designed to be flexible in use. Links are made on each page to activities in the companion teachers' book, *Developing Mental Maths with 7–9 year olds*, from which these photocopiable activities follow. However, these activities will also stand alone; the teachers' notes for each indicate the key mental strategies that are being developed and that should have been introduced beforehand. The activities can be used independently for group work during a class numeracy hour; this will allow the teacher to give more support to another group. The activities provide sound practice in number skills, and could thus be used to enrich a school's maths scheme or as selected homework activities. The teachers' notes indicate ways in which the activity sheets can be modified to provide differentiation and further work; this may involve changing the numbers involved or changing the focus of the questions asked. You can also use the activity sheets provided as models for your own. These activities can be used in any order. A record sheet is given on page 32 to help with planning. It can be photocopied at A3 size for ease of use.

---

* *The Teaching and Assessment of Number at Key Stages 1–3*, Discussion Paper 10, March 1997, SCAA (Ma/97/762).

KEY FACTS REVIEW, PAGE 7

This can be used at the start of Year 3 to determine 'readiness' for the activities in this book, which build on the basic counting and calculation skills tested here. Afterwards, discuss the children's strategies – for example, did they count on or use number bonds to solve question 10? The page can be photocopied, or the test can be administered to groups orally. In either case, the children should be given sufficient time to answer, since this is not intended as a test of speed. If you are reading out the questions, keep a record of the language you use (such as 'multiply by' or 'times') and note which words the children recognise.

ANSWERS: 1. 11, 15, 28, 43, 50, 104. **2.** 4, 7, 9, 17, 30. **3.** 13, 30, 31, 33, 103. **4.** Two of 23, 24, 25 and 26. **5.** Two of 99, 100, 101 and 102. **6.** Various. **7.** Various. **8.** 31. **9.** 37. **10.** 20. **11.** 13. **12.** 8, 14, 10, 8. **13.** 12. **14.** 50. **15.** 7. **16.** 5.

COUNTING & ORDERING

THE MISSING NUMBERS, PAGE 8

The children should be familar with the layout of a 100 square, and could use one to check their answers. These puzzles will work with either a 1–100 square or a 0–99 square. After completing this sheet, children could play the board game 'The great cover-up' (see *Developing Mental Maths with 7–9 year olds*, p.19).

KEY STRATEGY: the child needs to realise that the difference horizontally between two consecutive numbers is always 1, and the difference vertically is always 10.

MODIFY THE SHEET BY: deleting some numbers before copying the page, to leave only one starting number (for more able children). Allow less confident children to refer to a 100 square throughout.

ANSWERS: 1. 46, 57. **2.** 24, 25, 33. **3.** 16, 27. **4.** 11, 22, 31, 32. **5.** 54, 64, 65. **6.** 28, 38, 47. **7.** 34, 44, 55. **8.** 39, 49, 58. **9.** 17, 35.

ALL THE NUMBERS, PAGE 9

Let the children initially write the digits on three cards or pieces of paper and move them around to get a 'feel' for the problem.

KEY STRATEGY: the child needs to realise that the value of a digit depends on its place; thus for the largest number, the largest digit needs to go in the 'hundreds' and the smallest in the 'units'. The child should also see that with three different digits, there will always be six different answers.

MODIFY THE SHEET BY: including a 0 as one of the digits; having two digits the same.

ANSWERS: Set 1. 632, 623, 362, 326, 263, 236. **Set 2.** 751, 715, 571, 517, 175, 157.

FIVE LINES, PAGE 10

As preparation, the children should practise counting in 5s from any number. (This works well as a whole-class circle game.)

KEY STRATEGY: the child should identify the units digit patterns, starting with the familiar '0 – 5 – 0 – 5' pattern (questions 1 to 4) and going on to other alternating number patterns (questions 5 to 10).

MODIFY THE SHEET BY: asking less confident children to count in 10s. More able children can practise counting in 3s and 4s from any starting number, including numbers greater than 100.

ANSWERS: 1. 25. **2.** 80. **3.** 45. **4.** 25. **5.** 38. **6.** 32. **7.** 58. **8.** 36. **9.** 54. **10.** 103.

THE NEAREST TEN, PAGE 11

The children could write the numbers on small self-adhesive notes and place them on a large 0–100 number line before writing on the sheet.

KEY STRATEGY: the child needs to realise that whether the number should be 'rounded up' or 'rounded down' depends on the units digit. On a number line, the position of a number determines whether it should be rounded up or down. If the units digit is 5, the convention is to round up.

MODIFY THE SHEET BY: including a third set of boxes alongside the number line and asking children to find further numbers that approximate to each of the tens. More able children could work with larger numbers, rounding to the nearest hundred.

ANSWERS: 20, 50, 90, 70, 60, 10, 30, 80, 100, 40.

SORT THE SUMS, PAGE 12

The children could work in pairs, reading out the sums to each other.

KEY STRATEGY: the child should realise (in advance of the final reflection questions) that two single-digit numbers will never total more than 18, while two two-digit numbers will always total at least 20. Getting a feel for the size of an answer is a key aid to mental calculation.

MODIFY THE SHEET BY: for more able children, include subtraction questions such as 25 – 7 and 47 – 10.

ANSWERS: Less than 20 8 + 7, 3 + 5, 6 + 3, 5 + 6, 11 + 4, 2 + 12. **Greater than 20** 15 + 15, 16 + 10, 9 + 15, 18 + 16, 10 + 20, 17 + 8.

CHOCOLATE FOR ALL, PAGE 13

The children could cut out the strips in order to make a clearer direct comparison.

KEY STRATEGY: the child should make links between the visual image (the strip) and the mathematical relationship of numerator and denominator. For example, $\frac{3}{4}$ of a strip is longer (visually) than $\frac{1}{2}$; and $\frac{1}{2}$ is mathematically equivalent to $\frac{2}{4}$, which is less than $\frac{3}{4}$. The strips provide a link between the 'parts of a whole' model of fractions encountered in the early years and a 'points on a number line model':

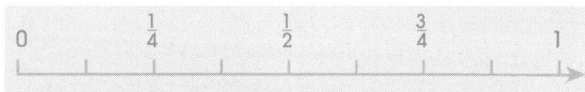

MODIFY THE SHEET BY: adding a bar divided into sixteenths and asking the children to set their own questions. Questions where the answer is 'the same' (for example, '$\frac{1}{4}$ or $\frac{2}{8}$?') could also be included.

ANSWERS: 1. A. **2.** B. **3.** A. **4.** A. **5.** B. **6.** B. **7.** B **8.** A. **9.** A. **10.** B.

ADDITION & SUBTRACTION

CHANGES, PAGE 14

These problems can be modelled using base 10 blocks, an abacus or a set of arrow cards. After completing this sheet, children could play the dice game 'Tens or units' (see *Developing Mental Maths with 7–9 year olds*, p.33).

KEY STRATEGY: the child should add or subtract the hundreds, tens or units digit as appropriate.

MODIFY THE SHEET BY: having a smaller number of steps before the final answer, or filling in one or two of the answers along the way (for less confident children). More able children could tackle problems where bridging of tens or hundreds is required (for example, starting with 387 and adding 30).

ANSWERS: Final numbers 797, 595, 660, 440, 0, 444.

THREESOME, PAGE 15

The children could start with a large card triangle and 23 cubes, moving the cubes around on the triangle and returning them to the centre each time.

KEY STRATEGY: the child should use the triangle image and mental calculation of doubles to regroup the numbers.

MODIFY THE SHEET BY: changing the target number. Targets above 30 should challenge more able children, who could also explore the patterns in a systematic listing of solutions (see below). Younger or less able children may need more experience with cubes or counters, or could work with smaller target numbers. The five triangles for each question on the worksheet are intended to represent an 'achievable minimum' for all the children.

ANSWERS: For 23 1,1, 21; 2, 2, 19; 3, 3, 17; 4, 4, 15; 5, 5, 13; 6, 6, 11; 7, 7, 9; 8, 8, 7; 9, 9, 5; 10, 10, 3; 11, 11, 1. **For 28** 1, 1, 26; 2, 2, 24; 3, 3, 22; 4, 4, 20; 5, 5, 18; 6, 6, 16; 7, 7,14; 8, 8, 12; 9, 9, 10; 10, 10, 8; 11, 11, 6; 12, 12, 4; 13, 13, 2.

FIND YOUR WAY AROUND, PAGE 16

The children could lay counters out on a larger 100 square before recording on the sheet. They will need a 100 square each for the extension task.

KEY STRATEGY: the child should use compensation methods for adding 9 (add 10, then take away 1: down one, then back one on the grid) and adding 11 (add 10, then add 1 (down one, then forward one on the grid). Children should be discouraged from counting on (as if playing 'Snakes and Ladders').

MODIFY THE SHEET BY: changing the steps to 'add 8' or 'add 12'. Alternatively, you could make up similar problems that involve starting at the bottom of the grid and then subtracting (for example, subtracting 9 by subtracting 10 and then adding 1).

ANSWERS: 1. 83. **2.** 98. **3.** 83. **4.** 98.

CHAINS, PAGE 17

A calculator or a number line will be useful for checking these problems.

KEY STRATEGY: as well as identifying the number sequences, the children will practise bridging and compensation strategies for adding and subtracting single-digit numbers.

MODIFY THE SHEET BY: asking the children to continue the chain until they have passed a particular number, such as 50 or 100. For less confident children, provide chains where there is only one operation. More able children can look at chains such as 'take away 4, add 3', which will lead naturally to work on negative numbers.

ANSWERS: 1. Take away 4, then add 5. **2.** Take away 3, then add 7. **3.** Add 7, then add 2. **4.** Add 8, then take away 4.

BALANCING ACT, PAGE 18

The children should be given opportunities to work with a real twin-pan balance or equaliser before attempting this task.

KEY STRATEGY: the child needs to regroup numbers in order to make the same totals in

different ways. This is a useful complement to the more usual 'a + b = ?' type of arithmetic, and helps to demonstrate the function of the equals sign.

MODIFY THE SHEET BY: increasing the magnitude of the weights on each side. More able children could also consider problems in which two weights on one side balance three weights on the other.

ANSWERS: 1. 25g. **2.** 20g. **3.** 18g. **4.** 25g. **5.** 15g. **6.** 17g.

ON THE SHELF, PAGE 19

It would be helpful for the children to have real coins to handle as they undertake this activity.

KEY STRATEGY: the child needs to carry out quick mental addition in the context of money, and to use the decimal point when recording amounts greater than £1.

MODIFY THE SHEET BY: replacing the £1 coin with 1p for children who are not confident with amounts greater than £1. For more able children, allow each coin to be used more than once, or allow for combinations of four or more different coins; either of these amendments will greatly expand the range of possible answers.

ANSWERS: with six different coins, there are 15 different two-coin combinations and 20 different three-coin ones.

THREE DARTS, PAGE 20

It will be useful for the children to have an A4-sized copy of the dartboard for this activity (see *Developing Mental Maths with 7–9 year olds*, photocopiable page 61) and three counters, so that combinations can be tried out before recording. After completing the sheet, children could play the dice and cards game 'Target 21' (see *Developing Mental Maths with 7–9 year olds*, p.34).

KEY STRATEGY: the child needs to regroup and combine numbers in a methodical way.

MODIFY THE SHEET BY: adjusting the range of numbers on the board, as well as the target number, to simplify or extend the task. A dart can be allowed to fall in the same section as another dart, or to miss the board. Children can be encouraged to create their own variations.

ANSWERS: Ways of making 12 8, 3, 1; 7, 4, 1; 7, 3, 2; 6, 5, 1; 6, 4, 2; 5, 4, 3. **Ways of making 11** 8, 2, 1; 7, 3, 1; 6, 4, 1; 6, 3, 2; 5, 4, 2.

TRIPLE JUMP, PAGE 21

This activity is an open-ended problem of the type ☐ + ☐ + ☐ = 20 within a visual context.

KEY STRATEGY: the child needs to perform quick mental addition of three numbers.

MODIFY THE SHEET BY: reducing the range of possible answers by imposing extra restrictions on

the frog, such as 'No jump is less than 3m' or 'No jump is greater than 10m'. Less confident children can start with a smaller total (such as 15m); more able children can plan the jumps of a 'super-super-frog' which can manage 30m or 40m in three jumps.

GOING UP! PAGE 22

This activity provides an opportunity to work with a vertical number line which models a real situation.

KEY STRATEGY: the child needs to use bridging and partitioning methods for adding and subtracting, and to understand the relationship between the two operations.

MODIFY THE SHEET BY: providing simpler examples where the lift stops only at multiples of 5 and 10. For more able children, extending the floors below ground level would be a good way to model negative numbers.

ANSWERS: 1. 7, 8, 5, 13, 17. **2.** 10, 15, 10, 8, 7. **3.** 3, 8, 20, 12, 7. **4.** 5, 13, 8, 17, 7.

MULTIPLICATION & DIVISION

PATTERN MAKER, PAGE 23

As preparation for this activity, count around the class (or group) in multiples of the numbers 2 to 5, starting at 2, 3, 4 or 5 respectively and going up to 40 (at least).

KEY STRATEGY: the child needs to recognise patterns in multiples – for example, multiples of 2 are even, while multiples of 3 are alternatively odd and even.

MODIFY THE SHEET BY: providing 100 squares, so the children can record multiples up to 100. Able children could mark multiples of two numbers (such as 2 and 5) on one grid, noting common multiples.

FIND THE CONNECTIONS, PAGE 24

Children should revise times tables before working on this activity. After completing the sheet, they could play the card game 'Stake a claim' (see *Developing Mental Maths with 7–9 year olds*, p.48).

KEY STRATEGY: the child needs to be aware that multiplication is commutative (A × B = B × A), and

that division is the inverse of multiplication (if
$A \times B = C$ then $C \div A = B$ and $C \div B = A$).
MODIFY THE SHEET BY: allowing children to
continue using numbers of their choice. They could
also focus on a single times table – for example,
writing out the 4 times table with the commutative
equivalents and complementary division bonds
alongside.

QUESTION TIME, PAGE 25
This activity provides opportunities to contextualise
number bonds.
KEY STRATEGY: the child needs to understand
and use the language of multiplication and
division (see page 6).
MODIFY THE SHEET BY: working through the
example orally with less confident children. Able
children can be asked to make up further
multiplication and division problems without the
number sentences to prompt them.
ANSWERS: $18 \div 2 = 9$ (9 conkers); $5 \times 4 = 20$ (20p).

WHICH IS MORE? PAGE 26
The children may prefer to model the problems
with cubes or counters. After completing this sheet,
they could play the dice and board game 'High
and low' (see *Developing Mental Maths with 7–9
year olds*, p.49).
KEY STRATEGY: the child needs to connect
doubling/halving and trebling/finding thirds with
the 2 and 3 times tables respectively.
MODIFY THE SHEET BY: extending to include
examples of '4 times' and 'a quarter of'.
ANSWERS: 1. Twice 6. **2.** Double 9. **3.** Half of 18.
4. The same. **5.** Double 8. **6.** Treble 6. **7.** Twice 11.
8. Half of 50.

RECTANGLES, PAGE 27
The children could draw the rectangles (and
further examples) on squared paper. The rectangle
provides a strong visual image of multiplication.
KEY STRATEGY: the child should find the number
of squares by multiplying the numbers of rows and
columns, rather than by counting the squares.
MODIFY THE SHEET BY: asking the children to
draw further rectangles on squared paper and
find pairs with the same area.
ANSWERS: the pairs are A and G, B and E, C and
H, D and F.

MULTISTEP & MIXED OPERATIONS

CARD COMBINATIONS, PAGE 28
Playing cards (or photocopies of them) should be
available for the children to use if they wish.
KEY STRATEGY: the child needs reasoning and
checking skills, as well as the ability to use multiples
in various combinations.
MODIFY THE SHEET BY: starting with different
pairs of numbers – for example, 2s and 3s or 2s and
5s (simpler), or 4s and 5s or 5s and 6s (more difficult).
Note that with two even numbers, only even-
numbered totals are possible.

INS AND OUTS, PAGE 29
Read through the questions with the children
initially, to help them recognise the operations.
KEY STRATEGY: in order to perform two successive
operations, the children should hold the interim
number in their heads. They should check their
answers by using the inverse operations.
MODIFY THE SHEET BY: having only multiplication
and addition functions (to make the activity
simpler). Extend the activity by increasing the range
of 'IN' numbers, or by having a third box with a
further operation.
ANSWERS: 2. 17. **3.** 21. **4.** 22. **5.** 35. **6.** 27. **7.** 16. **8.** 9.
9. 4. **10.** 7.

SPIDER ARITHMETIC, PAGE 30
This activity requires the children to 'find questions'
for a given answer.
KEY STRATEGY: the child needs to start with a
number smaller than the target for addition and
multiplication, and start with a number larger than
the target for subtraction and division.
MODIFY THE SHEET BY: limiting the number of
different operations used or lowering the target
number (simpler), or increasing the target number
(more difficult).

ON A BUDGET, PAGE 31
Provide real 1p, 2p and 5p coins for the children.
KEY STRATEGY: the children need to use multiples
in various combinations. They should check their
work by using inverse operations.
MODIFY THE SHEET BY: giving less money to
spend and limiting purchases to one or none of
each item. Extend the activity by increasing the
amount of spending money and adding new items
of confectionery.
ANSWERS: 1. No. **2.** Yes. **3.** Yes. **4.** Yes. **5.** No. **6.** Yes.
7. No. **8.** Yes. **9.** Yes.

MATHS WORDS LIST

above	go up	pounds
addition	greater than	quarter
approximately	group	round down
balance	half	round up
below	horizontal	share
coins	hundreds	subtraction
combine	in between	sum
decrease	increase	tens
difference	less than	third
digit	multiple	thousands
division	multiplication	times
double	number	treble
eighth	odd	twice
equal	pattern	units
even	pence	value
go down	place order	vertical

NAME   DATE

KEY FACTS REVIEW

1. What is 5 more than:

6 _____

10 _____

23 _____

38 _____

45 _____

99 _____

2. What is 3 less than:

7 _____

10 _____

12 _____

20 _____

33 _____

3. Put these numbers in order of size:

31,   103,   13,   33,   30

_____

4. Write down two numbers that come between 22 and 27.

_____   _____

5. Write down two numbers that come between 98 and 103.

_____   _____

6. Find two ways to make 15 using addition:

☐ + ☐ = 15   ☐ + ☐ = 15

7. Find two ways to make 6 using subtraction:

☐ – ☐ = 6   ☐ – ☐ = 6

8. $16 + 15 =$ ☐

9. $42 - 5 =$ ☐

10. $4 + 7 + 6 + 3 =$ ☐

11. $20 - 2 - 5 =$ ☐

12. What is: double 4? _____

double 7? _____

half of 20? _____

half of 16? _____

13. $3 \times 4 =$ ☐

14. $5 \times 10 =$ ☐

15. $35 \div 5 =$ ☐

16. $15 \div 3 =$ ☐

THE MISSING NUMBERS

These grids are all pieces of a 100 square.
■ See if you can work out the missing numbers.

1.

	47
56	

2.

23		
		35

3.

	17

4.

	12
21	

5.

63	
	74

6.

27	
	48

7.

	35
54	

8.

48	
	59

9.

26	
	37

■ Use squared paper to make some puzzles like these for a friend.

✏ What do you notice about any two numbers that are next to each other **horizontally**? What do you notice about any two numbers that are next to each other **vertically**? Write on the back of the sheet.

ALL THE NUMBERS

■ How many different numbers can you make with these three digits? You can only use each digit once in each number.

| 3 | 6 | 2 |

■ Arrange your answers from the largest to the smallest:

_____ _____ _____ _____ _____ _____

Largest   **Smallest**

■ Now do the same with these three digits:

| 7 | 1 | 5 |

_____ _____ _____ _____ _____ _____

Largest   **Smallest**

■ Now choose your own three numbers to try:

_____ _____ _____ _____ _____ _____

Largest   **Smallest**

How did you put the numbers in order?

On the back of the sheet, write about how you decided the order.

SEE *DEVELOPING MENTAL MATHS WITH 7–9 YEAR OLDS* 'CALL THE CARDS' P.12, 'THE THREE-CARD SHUFFLE' P.17

PRACTISING MENTAL MATHS

FIVE LINES

■ On each of these number lines, the numbers go up in 5s. Find the number that goes in the empty box.

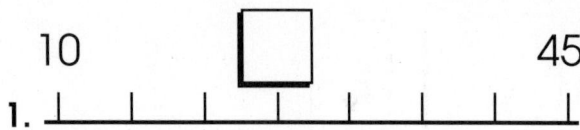

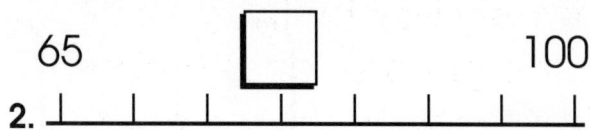

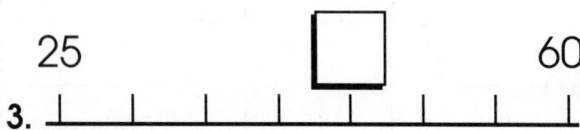

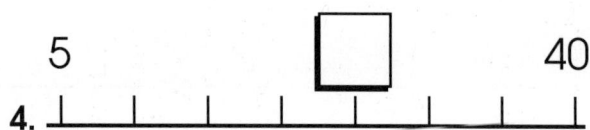

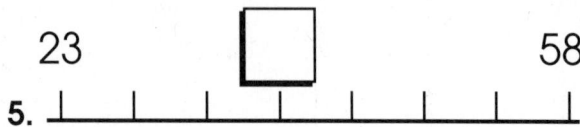

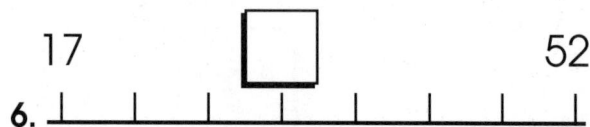

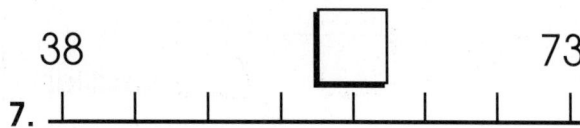

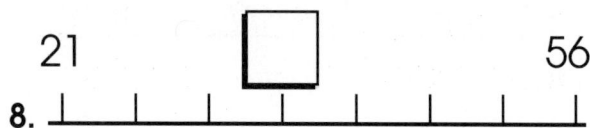

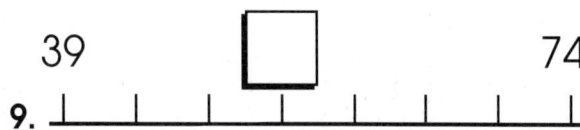

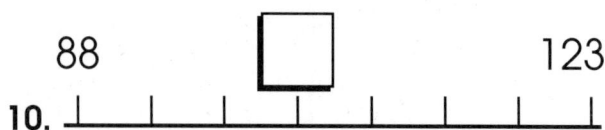

1. 10 ☐ 45

2. 65 ☐ 100

3. 25 ☐ 60

4. 5 ☐ 40

5. 23 ☐ 58

6. 17 ☐ 52

7. 38 ☐ 73

8. 21 ☐ 56

9. 39 ☐ 74

10. 88 ☐ 123

Check your answers with a friend.

Which was the easiest answer to find? Which was the hardest? Explain why on the back of this sheet.

SEE *DEVELOPING MENTAL MATHS WITH 7–9 YEAR OLDS* 'THE TRIPWIRE' P.13

THE NEAREST TEN

■ Round each of the following numbers to the nearest ten. Write it in an empty box by the appropriate tens number on the scale on the right. The first two have been done for you.

23	12
48	29
91	75
67	99
62	36

■ Now fill in each empty box with another number that would approximate to that ten. For example, in the box next to 23, you could put 19 or 22.

On the back of this sheet, write some instructions for a friend who has been away, explaining how to round numbers to the nearest ten.

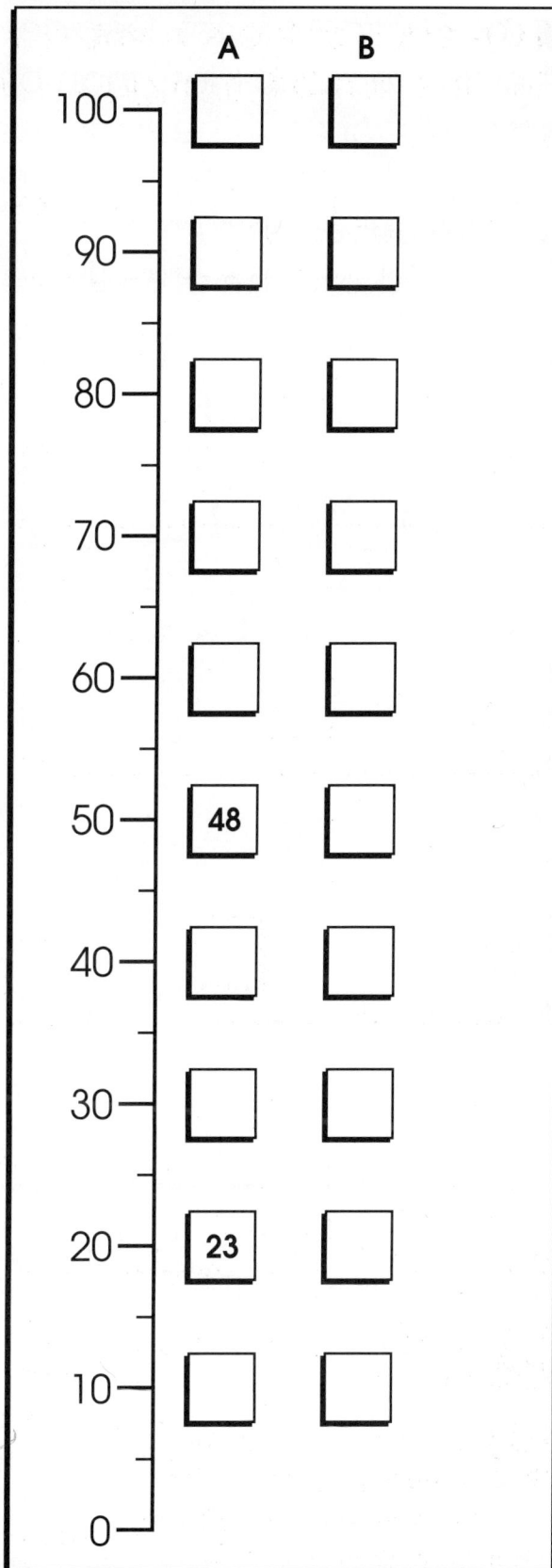

	A	B
100		
90		
80		
70		
60		
50	48	
40		
30		
20	23	
10		
0		

40 50 60

SEE DEVELOPING MENTAL MATHS WITH 7–9 YEAR OLDS 'FIND THE NEAREST...' P.14

COUNTING AND ORDERING

NAME

DATE

SORT THE SUMS

■ Look at these sums. Decide as quickly as you can whether the answer will be less than or greater than 20. (You don't have to work out the exact answer.)

■ Write out each sum in the appropriate part of the table below, adding the answers.

8 + 7	15 + 15	16 + 10	3 + 5
9 + 15	6 + 3	5 + 6	18 + 16
10 + 20	11 + 4	2 + 12	17 + 8

Answers less than 20 (< 20)	Answers greater than 20 (> 20)

■ Check your answers with a friend. Then make up three more sums for each column in the table.

💡 Why do two **single-digit** numbers never add up to more than 20? Why do two **two-digit** numbers always come to at least 20?

✏️ Explain in your own words on the back of this sheet.

SEE DEVELOPING MENTAL MATHS WITH 7–9 YEAR OLDS 'MAKE A CHOICE' P.14

NAME _____ **DATE** _____

CHOCOLATE FOR ALL

Three chocolate bars have been cut up into different-sized pieces: halves ($\frac{1}{2}$), quarters ($\frac{1}{4}$) and eighths ($\frac{1}{8}$) of a bar.

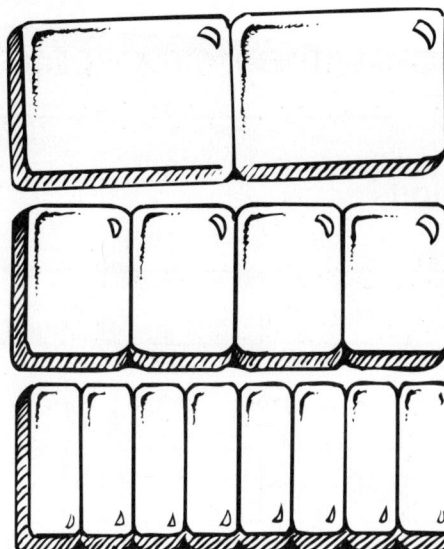

■ Write your name in box A and your friend's name in box B, then write in the third column who gets the biggest piece of chocolate each time.

	A	B	Who gets the biggest piece?
1.	$\frac{1}{2}$	$\frac{1}{4}$	
2.	$\frac{1}{8}$	$\frac{1}{4}$	
3.	$\frac{1}{2}$	$\frac{1}{8}$	
4.	$\frac{1}{2}$	$\frac{3}{8}$	
5.	$\frac{1}{2}$	$\frac{3}{4}$	
6.	$\frac{2}{4}$	$\frac{5}{8}$	
7.	$\frac{4}{8}$	$\frac{3}{4}$	
8.	$\frac{7}{8}$	$\frac{3}{4}$	
9.	$\frac{6}{8}$	$\frac{1}{2}$	
10.	$\frac{3}{8}$	$\frac{3}{4}$	

✏ On the back of the sheet, use chocolate bar drawings to prove your answers.

SEE DEVELOPING MENTAL MATHS WITH 7–9 YEAR OLDS 'THE BIGGEST PIECE' P.16

PRACTISING MENTAL MATHS

CHANGES

■ Follow the instructions to change each number.

Addition

Start   Finish

+ 10   + 100   + 3   + 20   + 300

| 364 | → | | → | | → | | → | | → | |

+ 100   + 20   + 200   + 5   + 50

| 220 | → | | → | | → | | → | | → | |

+ 200   + 10   + 100   + 10   + 300

| 40 | → | | → | | → | | → | | → | |

Subtraction

Start   Finish

– 10   – 200   – 7   – 100   – 20

| 777 | → | | → | | → | | → | | → | |

– 100   – 6   – 10   – 200   – 10

| 326 | → | | → | | → | | → | | → | |

– 10   – 200   – 40   – 5   – 300

| 999 | → | | → | | → | | → | | → | |

■ Check your 'Finish' numbers with a friend's. Do you agree? If not, you will both need to check carefully through the chain.

Which numbers were easy to add and subtract? Which were more difficult? Tell your friend.

SEE DEVELOPING MENTAL MATHS WITH 7–9 YEAR OLDS 'CARD CHANGES' P.22

THREESOME

The three numbers at the corners of the triangle must add up to the number in the centre, and two of the numbers must be the same.

5

23

9   9

■ Find some more solutions for 23. **Remember:** two of the numbers must be the same.

23   23   23   23   23

■ Now find some solutions for 28. **Remember:** two of the corner numbers must be the same.

28   28   28   28   28

Check your answers with a friend. Do you think that you have found all the possible answers between you? How do you know?

Explain how you know on the back of the sheet.

SEE DEVELOPING MENTAL MATHS WITH 7–9 YEAR OLDS 'TRIANGULATION' P.23 AND 'THREE-WAY SPLIT' P.31

ADDITION AND SUBTRACTION

ADDITION AND SUBTRACTION

FIND YOUR WAY AROUND

■ Shade in each start number and then follow the instructions, shading in each square that you land on.

1	2	3	4	5	6	7	8	9	10
11	12	13	14	15	16	17	18	19	20
21	22	23	24	25	26	27	28	29	30
31	32	33	34	35	36	37	38	39	40
41	42	43	44	45	46	47	48	49	50
51	52	53	54	55	56	57	58	59	60
61	62	63	64	65	66	67	68	69	70
71	72	73	74	75	76	77	78	79	80
81	82	83	84	85	86	87	88	89	90
91	92	93	94	95	96	97	98	99	100

1. **Start at 6**, add 9, add 10, add 9, add 11, add 10, add 9, add 9, add 10.
Finish number: _____

1	2	3	4	5	6	7	8	9	10
11	12	13	14	15	16	17	18	19	20
21	22	23	24	25	26	27	28	29	30
31	32	33	34	35	36	37	38	39	40
41	42	43	44	45	46	47	48	49	50
51	52	53	54	55	56	57	58	59	60
61	62	63	64	65	66	67	68	69	70
71	72	73	74	75	76	77	78	79	80
81	82	83	84	85	86	87	88	89	90
91	92	93	94	95	96	97	98	99	100

2. **Start at 17**, add 11, add 11, add 9, add 10, add 10, add 9, add 11, add 10.
Finish number: _____

1	2	3	4	5	6	7	8	9	10
11	12	13	14	15	16	17	18	19	20
21	22	23	24	25	26	27	28	29	30
31	32	33	34	35	36	37	38	39	40
41	42	43	44	45	46	47	48	49	50
51	52	53	54	55	56	57	58	59	60
61	62	63	64	65	66	67	68	69	70
71	72	73	74	75	76	77	78	79	80
81	82	83	84	85	86	87	88	89	90
91	92	93	94	95	96	97	98	99	100

3. **Start at 6**, add 9, add 10, add 9, add 11, add 10, add 9, add 9, add 10.
Finish number: _____

1	2	3	4	5	6	7	8	9	10
11	12	13	14	15	16	17	18	19	20
21	22	23	24	25	26	27	28	29	30
31	32	33	34	35	36	37	38	39	40
41	42	43	44	45	46	47	48	49	50
51	52	53	54	55	56	57	58	59	60
61	62	63	64	65	66	67	68	69	70
71	72	73	74	75	76	77	78	79	80
81	82	83	84	85	86	87	88	89	90
91	92	93	94	95	96	97	98	99	100

4. **Start at 17**, add 11, add 11, add 9, add 10, add 10, add 9, add 11, add 10.
Finish number: _____

Explain to your friend a quick way to add 9, 10 or 11 to a number.

Using a clean 100 square, make up a similar problem for a friend.

SEE DEVELOPING MENTAL MATHS WITH 7–9 YEAR OLDS 'THIS WAY AND THAT' P.24 AND 'MORE OR LESS' P.25

CHAINS

■ Each of these number chains has a rule. Complete each number chain and explain underneath it what the rule is.

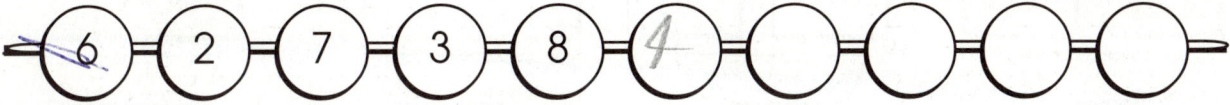

1. Rule _____

2. Rule _____

3. Rule _____

4. Rule _____

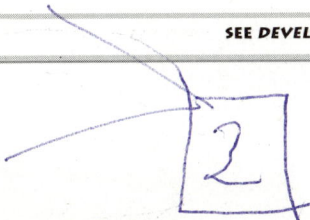 Now make up some number chains of your own. Write down the chains and the rules on separate pieces of paper. Ask a friend to work out what the rules are.

SEE *DEVELOPING MENTAL MATHS WITH 7–9 YEAR OLDS* 'ADD THIS, TAKE THAT' P.26

NAME   DATE

BALANCING ACT

■ Find the weight needed to make each of these scales balance.

1. | 20g | 10g | | | 5g | 2. | 25g | 10g | | 15g | |

3. | | 12g | | 15g | 15g | 4. | 25g | | | 15g | 35g |

5. | 20g | 22g | | | 27g | 6. | 49g | | | 31g | 35g |

■ For each of the scales below, choose two weights to put on each side so that the two sides balance. You **must** put a different set of weights on each side!

🖉 Write some instructions for a friend, telling her or him how to check that the two sides balance. Use the reverse side of this sheet.

SEE DEVELOPING MENTAL MATHS WITH 7–9 YEAR OLDS 'FIND THE BALANCE' P.27

ON THE SHELF

■ Imagine you are a shopkeeper who has to mark a range of prices on items in the shop. Each item must go on sale at a different price. You must be able to make up each price exactly with two or three different coins.

■ Write a possible price, and the coins that can be used to make it, under each item below. One example has been done for you.

Cost– 32p
Use – 20p 10p 2p

■ When you have finished, swap sheets with a friend and check each other's answers.

Can you and your friend agree on what the highest and lowest possible prices are?

Write an explanation of the highest and lowest prices on the reverse side of this sheet.

SEE DEVELOPING MENTAL MATHS WITH 7–9 YEAR OLDS 'THE STRANGE SWEETSHOP' P.27

THREE DARTS

Dartboard rules: In each turn, you have three darts to throw. The darts must land on different numbers.

■ On each board, show a possible score by ringing the three numbers landed on. Follow the instruction in each box.

Show four different ways of making 11 with three darts.

Show four different ways of making 12 with three darts.

Show two more **even** totals.

Show two more **odd** totals.

When you have finished, compare some of your friends' answers with your own. Are they the same?

Between you, have you found all the ways of making 11 or 12? How can you be sure? Write on the back of the sheet.

SEE DEVELOPING MENTAL MATHS WITH 7–9 YEAR OLDS 'DARTBOARD 1' P.28

NAME _____   DATE _____

TRIPLE JUMP

Ferdy the frog can always reach the end of the line in three hops. Here is one way he could do it:

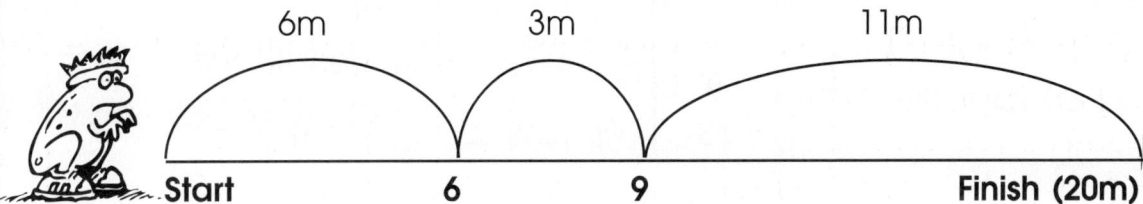

■ On these lines, mark some different sets of three jumps that Ferdy could make:

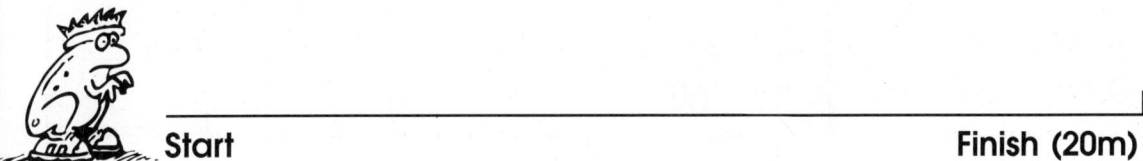

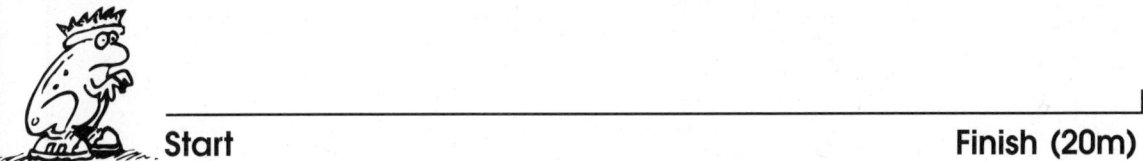

Frances the super-frog can manage 25 metres in three hops. Draw some of her possible sets of jumps on the lines below.

 Check your answers. Which are easy to check? Which are more difficult?

SEE DEVELOPING MENTAL MATHS WITH 7–9 YEAR OLDS 'FROG HOPS' P.28

NAME _____   DATE _____

GOING UP!

ADDITION AND SUBTRACTION

A lift travels from the ground floor (Floor 0) to the top of a skyscraper (Floor 50), stopping at four floors in between.

■ For each of the lift journeys shown below, write how many floors the lift goes up at each stage. The first three stages of journey 1 have been worked out for you. Start by checking these answers.

Check your answers with a friend.

Can you check by starting at 50 and going back down?

1.
50 — Up _____
33 — Up _____
20 — Up 5
15 — Up 8
7 — Up 7
0

2.
50 — Up _____
43 — Up _____
35 — Up _____
25 — Up _____
10 — Up _____
0

3.
50 — Up _____
43 — Up _____
31 — Up _____
11 — Up _____
3 — Up _____
0

4.
50 — Up _____
43 — Up _____
26 — Up _____
18 — Up _____
5 — Up _____
0

SEE DEVELOPING MENTAL MATHS WITH 7–9 YEAR OLDS 'STEPPING STONES' P.33

PATTERN MAKER

■ On each 1–60 grid, shade in the multiples of the number asked for using a coloured pencil or pen. Then describe any patterns you notice.

Multiples of 2

1	2	3	4	5	6	7	8	9	10
11	12	13	14	15	16	17	18	19	20
21	22	23	24	25	26	27	28	29	30
31	32	33	34	35	36	37	38	39	40
41	42	43	44	45	46	47	48	49	50
51	52	53	54	55	56	57	58	59	60

I noticed that

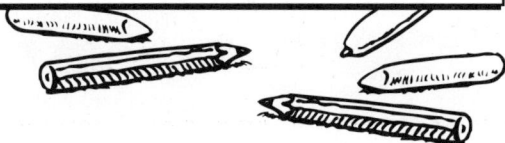

Multiples of 3

1	2	3	4	5	6	7	8	9	10
11	12	13	14	15	16	17	18	19	20
21	22	23	24	25	26	27	28	29	30
31	32	33	34	35	36	37	38	39	40
41	42	43	44	45	46	47	48	49	50
51	52	53	54	55	56	57	58	59	60

I noticed that

Multiples of 4

1	2	3	4	5	6	7	8	9	10
11	12	13	14	15	16	17	18	19	20
21	22	23	24	25	26	27	28	29	30
31	32	33	34	35	36	37	38	39	40
41	42	43	44	45	46	47	48	49	50
51	52	53	54	55	56	57	58	59	60

I noticed that

Multiples of 5

1	2	3	4	5	6	7	8	9	10
11	12	13	14	15	16	17	18	19	20
21	22	23	24	25	26	27	28	29	30
31	32	33	34	35	36	37	38	39	40
41	42	43	44	45	46	47	48	49	50
51	52	53	54	55	56	57	58	59	60

I noticed that

Why do you get these different patterns? Explain to your teacher.

SEE DEVELOPING MENTAL MATHS WITH 7–9 YEAR OLDS 'JUMPING UP THE LINE' P.38 AND 'COUNTERS ON A LINE' P.46

MULTIPLICATION AND DIVISION

FIND THE CONNECTIONS

■ Complete this table to show the connections between multiplication and division.

MULTIPLICATION AND DIVISION

	Multiply		Divide	
2, 4, 8	2 × 4 = 8	4 × 2 = 8	8 ÷ 2 = 4	8 ÷ 4 = 2
2, 6, 12	2 × 6 = 12	8 × 2 = 16	12 ÷ 2 = 6	
3, 4, 12	3 × 4 = 12	4 × 3 = 12		12 ÷ 4 = 3
2, 10, 20	2 × 10 = 20		20 ÷ 2 = 10	
3, 5, 15	3 × 5 = 15			
2, 8, 16	2 × 8 = 16	8 × 2 = 6		
5, 7, 35	5 × 7 = 35		35 ÷ 5 = 7	
3, 8, 24	3 × 8 = 24			24 ÷ 8 = 3
2, 7, 14	2 × 7 = 14			
5, 6, 30	5 × 6 = 30			
7, 10, 70	7 × 10 = 16			
3, 6, 18	3 × 6 = 18			

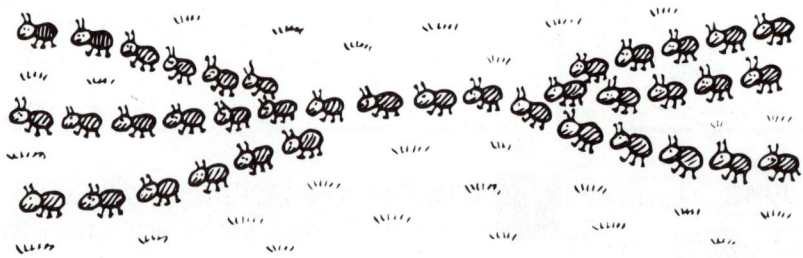

💡 Check your answers with a friend. Explain to your friend how multiplication and division are related.

SEE DEVELOPING MENTAL MATHS WITH 7–9 YEAR OLDS 'WHAT ELSE DO YOU KNOW?' P.39

QUESTION TIME

■ Write a number sentence for each of these questions, giving the answer.

> Two children share eighteen conkers. How many does each child have?

> How much will I pay for five sweets if each sweet costs 4p?

■ Now make up a question (in words) for each of these number sentences:

> $4 \times 6 = 24$

> $2 \times 8 = 16$

> $30 \div 5 = 6$

> $21 \div 3 = 7$

Which do you find easiest to make up: multiplication questions or division questions? Does your partner agree?

SEE DEVELOPING MENTAL MATHS WITH 7–9 YEAR OLDS 'GET IN GROUPS' P.40 AND 'ASK ME A QUESTION' P.42

WHICH IS MORE?

■ Can you tell me which is more?

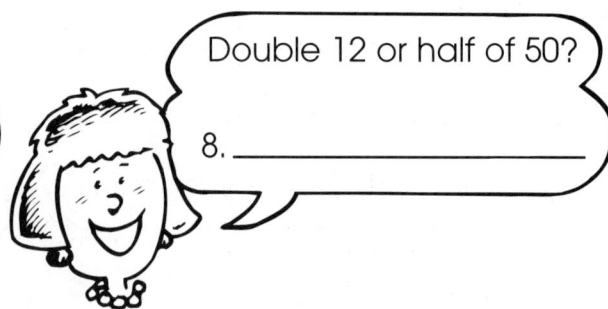

Twice 6 or half of 20?

1. _____

Treble 5 or double 8?

5. _____

Double 9 or a third of 30?

2. _____

Half of 30 or treble 6?

6. _____

A third of 24 or half of 18?

3. _____

Treble 7 or twice 11?

7. _____

Treble 4 or half of 24?

4. _____

Double 12 or half of 50?

8. _____

Check your answers with a friend. Can you prove to him or her that your answers are true?

Make up some more problems like these and write them on the back of the sheet. Can your friend solve them?

SEE *DEVELOPING MENTAL MATHS WITH 7–9 YEAR OLDS* 'YOU AND A FRIEND' P.42 AND 'HALF PRICE SALE' P.43

RECTANGLES

■ Draw lines to join rectangles that have the same number of squares.

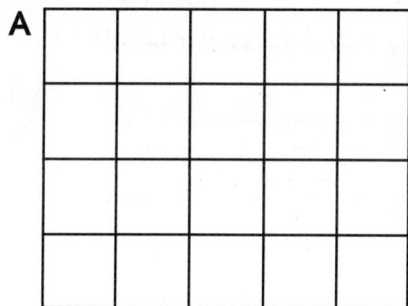

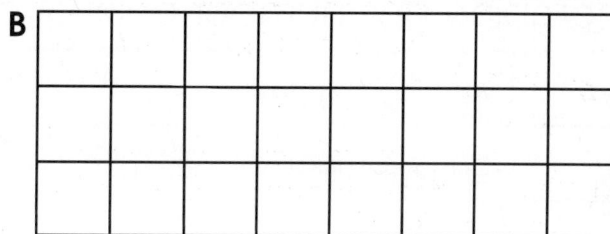

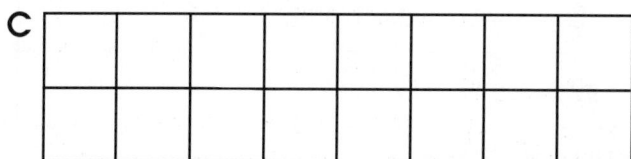

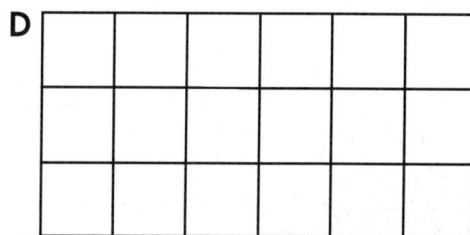

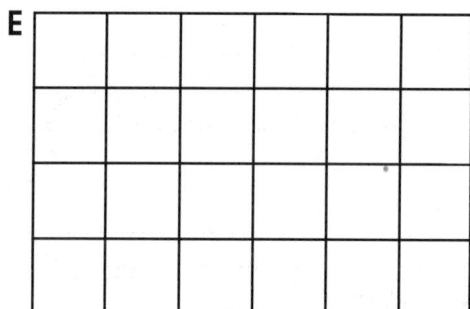

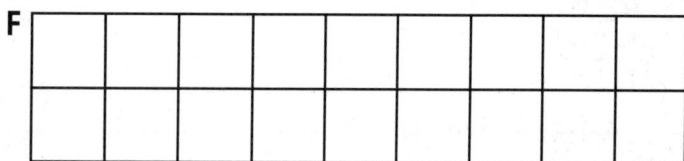

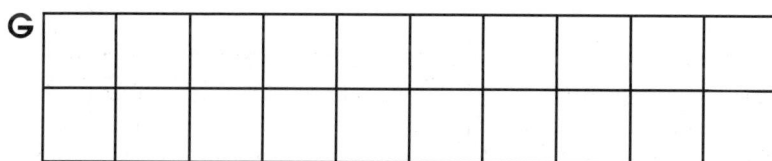

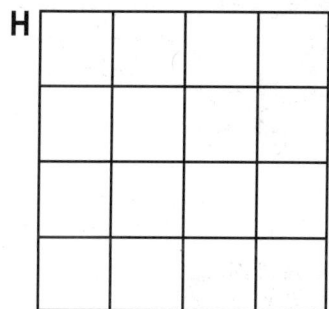

A

B

C

D

E

F

H

G

■ Now complete the number sentences below.

1. $3 \times 6 = \boxed{} \times \boxed{} = 18$ **3.** $4 \times 4 = \boxed{} \times \boxed{} = 16$

2. $4 \times 6 = \boxed{} \times \boxed{} = 24$ **4.** $2 \times 10 = \boxed{} \times \boxed{} = 20$

On the reverse side of this sheet, write some instructions to tell a friend who has been away how to pair up the rectangles.

SEE DEVELOPING MENTAL MATHS WITH 7–9 YEAR OLDS 'RECTANGLE AREAS' P.43 AND 'RECTANGULAR NUMBERS' P.46

MULTIPLICATION AND DIVISION

CARD COMBINATIONS

■ Complete the table below, showing a way to make each number from 6 to 40 using only 3s and/or 5s. You can combine any number of 3s and/or 5s.

6	Two 3s	24	
7	Can't be made	25	
8		26	
9		27	
10		28	Five 5s and one 3
11		29	
12		30	
13	Two 5s and one 3	31	
14		32	
15		33	
16		34	
17		35	
18		36	
19		37	
20		38	
21		39	
22		40	
23			

Compare your answers with your partner's answers. Did you use different ways of making some numbers?

SEE DEVELOPING MENTAL MATHS WITH 7–9 YEAR OLDS 'ALL THE THREES AND FOURS' P.52 AND 'MAKE UP THE NUMBERS' P.56

INS AND OUTS

■ Work out what the function boxes do to each of your **In** numbers. The first **Out** number has been written down for you.

1. In 4 $\boxed{\times 2}$ ⟶ $\boxed{+ 3}$ Out **11**

2. In 3 $\boxed{\times 5}$ ⟶ $\boxed{+ 2}$ Out _____

3. In 4 $\boxed{\times 4}$ ⟶ $\boxed{+ 5}$ Out _____

4. In 5 $\boxed{\times 3}$ ⟶ $\boxed{+ 7}$ Out _____

5. In 4 $\boxed{+ 3}$ ⟶ $\boxed{\times 5}$ Out _____

6. In 6 $\boxed{+ 3}$ ⟶ $\boxed{\times 3}$ Out _____

7. In 10 $\boxed{\div 2}$ ⟶ $\boxed{+ 11}$ Out _____

8. In 4 $\boxed{\times 5}$ ⟶ $\boxed{- 11}$ Out _____

9. In 12 $\boxed{+ 8}$ ⟶ $\boxed{\div 5}$ Out _____

10. In 21 $\boxed{- 7}$ ⟶ $\boxed{\div 2}$ Out _____

💡 Can you check your answers by starting with the **Out** number and working backwards?

✏️ Make up some similar problems for your friends to try. Write them on the back of this sheet.

SEE *DEVELOPING MENTAL MATHS WITH 7–9 YEAR OLDS* 'THE MAGIC BOXES' P. 54

SPIDER ARITHMETIC

■ For each spider, write one number sentence on each leg that gives the number on the spider's body. Try to use addition, subtraction, multiplication and division on different legs. One leg on each spider has been done for you.

10 + 5

15

20

40 ÷ 2

Swap your sheet with a friend. Check that each number sentence has the number on the spider as its answer.

Which is the easiest type of number problem to solve? Which is the most difficult type?

SEE DEVELOPING MENTAL MATHS WITH 7–9 YEAR OLDS 'THE MATHS OCTOPUS' P. 56

MULTISTEP AND MIXED OPERATIONS

ON A BUDGET

SWEET SHOP
Chews – 2p each
Gob stoppers – 3p each
Giant jellies – 4p each
Pink uglies – 5p each

■ You have 15p to spend. Do you have enough for

1. Three gob stoppers and two giant jellies?
2. One pink ugly and four chews?
3. One of each item?

■ You have 20p to spend. Do you have enough for

4. Three gob stoppers and two pink uglies?
5. Five chews and three giant jellies?
6. Four chews and two pink uglies?

■ You have 25p to spend. Do you have enough for

7. Two of each item?
8. Six gob stoppers and three chews?
9. Two pink uglies and five gob stoppers?

Now imagine you have 30p to spend. Make up two different lists of sweets that you could afford. Write them on the back of this sheet.

If you want to have as many sweets as possible, which are the best to choose? Which are the worst? Explain to your teacher.

SEE DEVELOPING MENTAL MATHS WITH 7–9 YEAR OLDS 'SWEETSHOP' P. 58

MULTISTEP AND MIXED OPERATIONS

TEACHERS' RECORD SHEET

NAMES	COUNTING & ORDERING						ADDITION & SUBTRACTION									MULTIPLICATION & DIVISION					MULTISTEP & MIXED OPERATIONS			
	THE MISSING NUMBERS, P8	ALL THE NUMBERS, P9	FIVE LINES, P10	THE NEAREST TEN, P11	SORT THE SUMS, P12	CHOCOLATE FOR ALL, P13	CHANGES, P14	THREESOME, P15	FIND YOUR WAY AROUND, P16	CHAINS, P17	BALANCING ACT, P18	ON THE SHELF, P19	THREE DARTS, P20	TRIPLE JUMP, P21	GOING UP! P22	PATTERN MAKER, P23	FIND THE CONNECTIONS, P24	QUESTION TIME, P25	WHICH IS MORE? P26	RECTANGLES, P27	CARD COMBINATIONS, P28	INS AND OUTS, P29	SPIDER ARITHMETIC, P30	ON A BUDGET, P31
1																								
2																								
3																								
4																								
5																								
6																								
7																								
8																								
9																								
10																								
11																								
12																								
13																								
14																								
15																								
16																								
17																								
18																								
19																								
20																								
21																								
22																								
23																								
24																								
25																								
26																								
27																								
28																								
29																								
30																								
31																								
32																								
33																								
34																								
35																								

PRACTISING MENTAL MATHS